GW01003519

Ransom Neutron Stars
The Last Soldier
by Stephen Rickard

Published by Ransom Publishing Ltd.
Unit 7, Brocklands Farm, West Meon, Hampshire GU32 1JN, UK
www.ransom.co.uk

ISBN   978 178591 451 5
First published in 2017

The Last Soldier

Stephen Rickard

Hiroo Onoda was born in Japan in 1922.

He came from a family of ancient samurai warriors.

His father had been a soldier too.

A samurai warrior, about 1860

Hiroo Onoda and his younger brother, 1944

In 1940, aged 18, Hiroo Onoda joined the Japanese Army.

He fought in the Second World War (1939 to 1945).

In 1944 the Japanese Army sent him to Lubang Island in the Philippines.

He joined a group of Japanese soldiers fighting against the Americans.

Japanese soldiers in the Philippines, 1942

The Japanese officers
told the men
to defend
Lubang Island.

The officers said,
"Never surrender."

In August 1945 the American Air Force dropped two atom bombs on Japan.

They dropped one bomb on the city of Hiroshima.

They dropped the second bomb
on the city of Nagasaki.

The two bombs killed
more than 225,000 people.

Nagasaki, September 1945.
Six weeks after the bomb

Six days later,
Japan surrendered.

The war was over.

Japan surrenders

On Lubang Island, Hiroo Onoda was hiding with three other Japanese soldiers.

They did not know that the war was over.

Nobody told them.

Lubang
Island

The Philippines

Two months later, in October 1945, Hiroo Onoda saw a leaflet dropped from an aircraft.

The leaflet said the war was over.

Hiroo Onoda thought it was a trick.

So he carried on fighting.

There was nobody left to fight,
but Hiroo Onoda stayed in hiding with
the three other Japanese soldiers.

They hid in the hills on Lubang Island.

They said, "The American army must
not capture us!"

In 1950, one of the men surrendered.
Now they were three.

In 1952 (seven years after the war
ended!) planes dropped letters and
family pictures on Lubang Island.

The letters asked the men to surrender.

The men still thought it was a trick.

They carried on fighting.

Then in 1954 one of the soldiers
was killed.

Now only two men were left.

Twenty-seven years after the war ended, in 1972, the soldier with Hiroo Onoda was killed.

Now Hiroo Onoda was alone.

He was still in hiding.

"Never surrender!"

In 1974 Hiroo Onoda met a fisherman called Norio Suzuki.

Norio Suzuki was looking for him.

Slowly the two men became friends –
but still Hiroo Onoda refused
to surrender.

He said he needed orders
from a Japanese officer.

So Norio Suzuki flew to Japan.

In Japan he found
Major Yoshimi Taniguchi.

He had been Hiroo Onoda's superior
officer in the war.

Then both men both flew
from Japan to Lubang Island.

They went to find Hiroo Onoda.

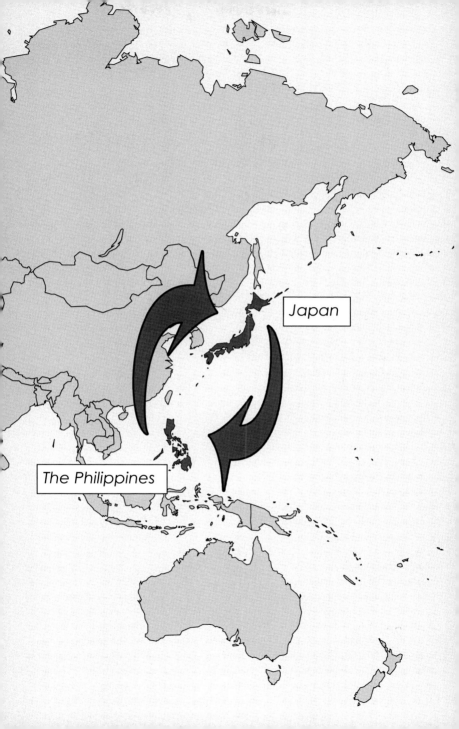

On March 9th, 1974
Major Yoshimi Taniguchi
met Hiroo Onoda on Lubang Island.

The major gave him his orders
to surrender.

Now Hiroo Onoda had his orders.

Twenty-nine years after the end
of the war, Hiroo Onoda surrendered.

He handed over his sword,
his rifle and ammunition,
and some hand grenades.

Two days later, on March 11th 1974,
he surrendered his sword
to President Marcos
of the Philippines.

For Hiroo Onoda,
at last the war was over.

Have you read?

Text Me

by Alice Hemming

Best Friends

by John Townsend

Ransom Neutron Stars

The Last Soldier
Word count **466**

Orange Book Band

Phonics

Phonics 1 Not Pop, Not Rock
Go to the Laptop Man
Gus and the Tin of Ham

Phonics 2 Deep in the Dark Woods
Night Combat
Ben's Jerk Chicken Van

Phonics 3 GBH
Steel Pan Traffic Jam
Platform 7

Phonics 4 The Rock Show
Gaps in the Brain
New Kinds of Energy

Book bands

Pink Curry!
Free Runners
My Toys

Red Shopping with Zombies
Into the Scanner
Planting My Garden

Yellow Fit for Love
The Lottery Ticket
In the Stars

Blue Awesome ATAs
Wolves
The Giant Jigsaw

Green Fly, May FLY!
How to Start Your Own
Crazy Cult
The Care Home

Orange Text Me
The Last Soldier
Best Friends